MAKE ME THE BEST

HOCKEY PLAYER

BY TODD KORTEMEIER

SportsZone

An Imprint of Abdo Publishing
abdopublishing.com

abdopublishing.com

Published by Abdo Publishing, a division of ABDO, PO Box 398166, Minneapolis, Minnesota 55439. Copyright © 2017 by Abdo Consulting Group, Inc. International copyrights reserved in all countries. No part of this book may be reproduced in any form without written permission from the publisher. SportsZone™ is a trademark and logo of Abdo Publishing.

Printed in the United States of America, North Mankato, Minnesota
092016
012017

Cover Photos: Robert Nyholm/Shutterstock Images, top left; Click Images/Shutterstock Images, top right; Shutterstock Images, middle left, bottom left; Nick Wass/AP Images, bottom right
Interior Photos: Robert Nyholm/Shutterstock Images, 4 (top); Shutterstock Images, 4 (middle), 4 (bottom); Click Images/Shutterstock Images, 4–5 (top); Nick Wass/AP Images, 4–5 (bottom); Keith Srakocic/AP Images, 6–7, 18–19, 20, 23, 25; Manuel Balce Ceneta/AP Images, 8; Luis M. Alvarez/AP Images, 11; Jeanine Leech/Icon Sportswire, 13; Michael Ainsworth/AP Images, 14; Joshua Sarner/Icon Sportswire, 17; Mark LoMoglio/Icon Sportswire, 26–27; John Hefti/Icon Sportswire, 28–29; Mark Zaleski/AP Images, 31; Keith Hamilton/Icon Sportswire, 33; Bob Frid/Icon Sportswire, 35; John Locher/AP Images, 36; Fred Kfoury III/Icon Sportswire, 39; John Crouch/Icon Sportswire, 41; Robin Alam/Icon Sportswire, 42; Keith Gillett/Icon Sportswire, 45

Editor: Patrick Donnelly
Series Designer: Nikki Farinella
Content Consultant: Jacob Mars, director, High Performance 14 Boys Program, Minnesota Hockey

Publisher's Cataloging-in-Publication Data

Names: Kortemeier, Todd, author.
Title: Make me the best hockey player / by Todd Kortemeier.
Description: Minneapolis, MN : Abdo Publishing, 2017. | Series: Make me the best
    athlete | Includes bibliographical references and index.
Identifiers: LCCN 2016945587 | ISBN 9781680784893 (lib. bdg.) | ISBN
    9781680798173 (ebook)
Subjects: LCSH: Hockey--Juvenile literature.
Classification: DDC 796.962--dc23
LC record available at http://lccn.loc.gov/2016945587

TABLE OF

CONTENTS

INTRODUCTION   **4**

SHOOT A WRIST SHOT LIKE
ALEX OVECHKIN   **6**

PLAY GOALIE LIKE
BEN BISHOP   **12**

SKATE LIKE
SIDNEY CROSBY   **18**

SHOOT A SLAP SHOT LIKE
SHEA WEBER   **26**

PLAY DEFENSE LIKE
DREW DOUGHTY   **34**

STICKHANDLE LIKE
PATRICK KANE   **40**

                                                      46
GLOSSARY   **47**
FOR MORE INFORMATION   **48**
INDEX/ABOUT THE AUTHOR

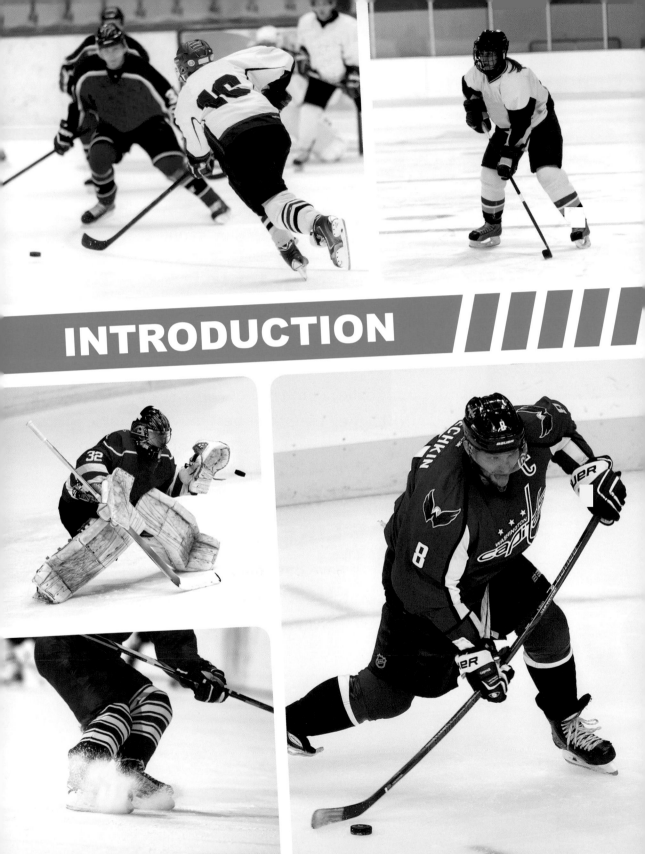

INTRODUCTION

Before they played in 20,000-seat arenas, they practiced on frozen ponds. Most of today's greatest hockey players started out as kids carving up outdoor ice rinks. They had early-morning practices and long road trips. Before faking out goalies in the National Hockey League (NHL), they tried their best moves on their friends and neighbors. Every blistering slap shot and punishing hit today is the result of all that work long ago.

Every star's journey is different, but they all have one thing in common. They all had to work hard to become the best hockey player.

SHOOT A WRIST SHOT LIKE

ALEX OVECHKIN

With the puck on his stick, Alex Ovechkin is the most dangerous player in the NHL. He gets up to speed quickly, then uses his size and speed to drive toward the net. A defenseman goes into a slide to try to block his shot. But Ovechkin waits for the defender to skid past him, then fires a wicked wrist shot. He's picked out his target perfectly. It's another goal for Ovechkin.

//////////// **During his first 11 NHL seasons, Ovechkin led the league in goals six times.**

Ovechkin grew up in Russia. He idolized NHL players such as Mario Lemieux. He dreamed of playing in the same league someday. The Washington Capitals chose Ovechkin first overall in the 2004 NHL draft. In his first season he scored 52 goals and won the Calder Memorial Trophy as

Alex Ovechkin heads up the ice in the 2011 NHL Winter Classic.

the league's best rookie. He remains an All-Star and Most Valuable Player (MVP) candidate every year.

Ovechkin uses any method he can to score goals. But he's especially effective with his wrist shot. Rather than winding up like a slap shot, in a wrist shot a player keeps the puck on his stick the whole time. With a quick flick of the wrists, Ovechkin sends the puck flying at speeds approaching

Ovechkin won his third Hart Memorial Trophy, which is given to the league MVP, in 2012–13.

SHOOT A WRIST SHOT LIKE ALEX OVECHKIN

- Start with the puck on your stick blade, holding it a bit behind your body, with your weight on your back foot.

- Lean on your stick to make it bend and store up power.

- Sweep your stick forward and transfer your weight to your front foot, keeping your eyes on the target.

- Roll your wrists just before you release the puck to give it spin. The back of your lead hand should be facing the ceiling.

Ovechkin keeps his head up as he skates so he can see all of his options with the puck.

Ovechkin generates power with his wrist shot by leaning on his stick and shifting his weight.

60 miles per hour (97 km/h). If he shoots within 15 feet (4.6 m) of the net, the goalie usually can't react in time to stop it.

Ovechkin has a lightning-quick release on his "wrister." He can wait until the exact moment he wants to shoot. He prefers his stick blade to have as much curve as possible to help him keep possession. As he releases the puck, he gives it a spin that makes it fly straighter. A wrister isn't as fast as a slap shot, but if it's accurate it's hard to stop.

JOE SAKIC

Joe Sakic retired in 2009 after playing 20 seasons with the Quebec Nordiques and the Colorado Avalanche. His wrist shot was nearly impossible for goalies to stop. It was fast and accurate. Sakic focused on releasing his wrist shot as quickly as he could. He even got to the point where he could shoot it while still in his normal skating stride. Because the wrister could come at any time, it was impossible for the goalie to predict. Many of Sakic's 625 career goals came via that deadly shot.

DRILL DOWN!

This drill helps develop a proper follow-through on your wrist shot.

1. Stand about 10 feet from the boards.

2. Shoot your wrist shot at the boards over and over.

3. The puck should come straight back to you each time.

4. If the puck comes off at an angle, that means you're not following straight through your shot, so concentrate more on your follow-through.

PLAY GOALIE LIKE

BEN BISHOP

On a breakaway, it's just the goalie against the shooter. Goalie Ben Bishop relishes these one-on-one situations. He sets up in front of the crease, giving the opposing skater less of the net as a target. Then Bishop slowly backs up, protecting the opening of the net. At the last second, the skater cuts back across the face of goal, but Bishop reacts. He plucks the shot out of the air, making another big save for his team.

When Bishop made his NHL debut in 2008, he was the tallest goalie ever to play in the league. At 6 feet 7 inches (200 cm), he beat the previous height record by two inches. Bishop began his career with his hometown team, the St. Louis Blues. It took

Bishop broke the Lightning career records for shutouts and victories in 2015–16.

Ben Bishop is ready to make a big save for the Tampa Bay Lightning.

him awhile to establish himself in the league. He soared to stardom in 2013–14 when he became the starting goalie in his second season with the Tampa Bay Lightning.

Bishop's size is both a positive and a negative at times. He takes up a lot of the net. But when he moves his long

PLAY GOALIE LIKE BEN BISHOP

- Work on your skating. The better you skate, the more effective you'll be in getting to the puck. Focus on getting up quickly after hitting the ice and work on your side-to-side movements.

- Watch the puck at all times, even when it's not in your zone.

- Follow the puck as it hits you. If you give up a rebound, you need to know where it is so you can try to clear or cover it.

- Keep your shoulders square to the puck if at all possible. That will give the shooter the smallest possible target to shoot at.

- Be ready to bounce back. You're going to give up goals—even bad ones. You need to shrug those off and concentrate on stopping the next shot.

- Communicate. Let your defensemen know where the puck is or if you're being screened on a play.

Bishop keeps his shoulders square to the puck to give himself the best chance of stopping it.

limbs, he can leave holes open for players to target. Bishop counters this by playing at the edge of the crease and challenging shooters. He moves quickly to cut down angles and tries to keep his shoulders square to the puck.

Bishop plays a butterfly style. This is the most common goaltending style in the NHL today. To stop pucks, Bishop often drops to his knees and spreads out his leg pads. This makes the goalie resemble the shape of a butterfly. This helps Bishop smother lower shots. If there's a rebound, Bishop excels at getting back on his skates quickly to recover and make another save.

PATRICK ROY

Goalies who grew up learning the butterfly style have Patrick Roy to thank. Roy didn't invent the style, but he mastered it and made it popular. When Roy debuted with the Montreal Canadiens in 1985, goalies mostly played standing on their skates. But Roy changed the game, dropping to his knees and frustrating scorers. Roy also had a quick glove hand to defend against high shots.

DRILL DOWN!

Develop hand-eye coordination with this exercise.

1. Stand a few feet from a wall.

2. Wear your catching glove on one hand but leave your other hand bare.

3. Begin by throwing a tennis ball against the wall and catching it with your bare hand.

4. Then switch to catching it with your glove. Gradually speed up so you can do this as fast as possible.

SKATE LIKE

SIDNEY CROSBY

As Sidney Crosby moves up the ice, defenders struggle to stay with him. He's not the fastest player in the rink. He's not the strongest or the toughest, either. But Crosby is fast enough, strong enough, and tough enough that he won't get pushed off the puck easily. Crosby stays low and keeps the puck away from defenders. He's able to weave his way through other players. Crosby gathers the puck and glides around the net. Then he picks out a teammate and threads a perfect pass to him for a one-timer. It's a great example of why Crosby is the NHL's active leader in assists per game.

Crosby won the Hart Trophy as the NHL MVP in 2007 and 2014.

Crosby's talent was clear from a young age. When he was 14 years old, he scored 95 goals and had 98 assists

Sidney Crosby uses the edges of his skate blades to keep his balance as he fends off an opponent.

playing at the midget level in his home province of Nova Scotia, Canada. He had great hand and wrist control. He was deadly with the puck on his stick. But Crosby needed to work on his skating. That same year, he teamed up with a personal trainer. Crosby learned how to have the

Crosby won gold medals playing with Canada at the 2010 and 2014 Winter Olympics.

SKATE LIKE SIDNEY CROSBY

- Make sure your skates fit properly. You won't skate as well if your toes are crunched or your feet are moving around in the boot. Tie your skates tightly and keep them snug around your foot.

- Bend your front knee up to 90 degrees. The more you bend the front knee, the more power you'll get from stretching and pushing off with your back leg. Push back and out, riding the inside edge of your other skate.

- Follow through on your push. Don't glide or walk on the ice. Fully extend your push leg and get some power behind it.

- Keep your back straight and your head still.

- Work on using both the inside and outside edges of your blade.

It's important to be able to stop quickly and change directions when you're skating.

proper posture on his skates. That training helped him use the skate blade better, making him faster and stronger.

Every NHL team wanted Crosby. The Pittsburgh Penguins got him with the first pick in the 2005 draft. By his second season, he was an All-Star and MVP and he posted the most points in the NHL. Crosby helped the Penguins win the Stanley Cup in 2009 and 2016 and was named MVP of the 2016 Final.

BOBBY ORR

When Bobby Orr debuted with the Boston Bruins in 1966, a defenseman's role was pretty simple: play defense. They rarely scored goals. In fact, in 1966, no defenseman had scored at least 20 goals in a season in more than 20 years. Orr did it seven seasons in a row. Not only did he usually lead defensemen in scoring, he led the whole NHL in scoring twice. Orr was such an effective two-way player because of his skating. He was amazingly fast, but his long strides made his movements look effortless. Former teammates recall times when Orr caught up with a forward from as much as 15 feet behind. Orr caught him by surprise, took the puck, and started a play the other way.

Crosby is one of the smoothest skaters in the NHL.

Crosby has continued to work on his skating, even as an NHL star. Part of his training includes focusing on flexibility and strength. With all the turning and cutting involved in skating, it pays to be flexible. Crosby generates power with his legs. But his upper body stays mostly still, which helps him handle the puck smoothly. One of Crosby's favorite moves is the heel-to-heel turn. This move gives him a good view of the ice and allows him to make a pass or change direction and skate the other way.

At 19 years, 9 months old, Crosby was the youngest captain in NHL history.

Some players like their skate blades sharpened a certain way. Crosby uses both edges of his skates. He doesn't want to favor one edge over the other. Crosby's gliding ability helps him make good passes. If he can glide without losing a lot of speed, he can survey the ice and pick out a teammate for a pass.

DRILL DOWN!

Crosby works on using the inside edge of his skates with this drill.

1. Skate a short distance forward, then turn left, using only the inside edge of your right skate.

2. After completing the turn, take one stride and turn to the right, using only the inside edge of your left skate.

3. Repeat this process, making figure-eights on the ice.

SHOOT A SLAP SHOT LIKE

SHEA WEBER

While all eyes are watching the forwards passing the puck, Shea Weber waits. He's guarding the blue line, ready to defend if the other team gets the puck. But Weber's also ready to attack. If he can find some space to shoot, he's got a secret weapon ready. As the other team's defense hurries toward the puck, a forward sends a pass back to the blue line, where Weber is waiting. He brings his stick back and unleashes a cannon of a shot.

////////// **Weber led all NHL defensemen in goals scored by slap shot from 2010 through 2016.**

Sailing at well over 100 miles per hour (161 km/h), the puck rockets into the top corner of the net.

Weber had plenty of time to practice his slap shot as a boy in British Columbia. His father managed the local

Shea Weber follows through on a slap shot.

ice rink. Weber and his friends got to play there after the rink was closed. All that practice paid off when the Nashville Predators chose Weber in the second round of the 2003 NHL draft.

Weber helped Canada win the men's hockey gold medal at the Olympics in 2010 and 2014.

SHOOT A SLAP SHOT LIKE SHEA WEBER

- Hold the stick with your bottom hand at least halfway down the length of your stick. Try to find the spot where the stick is the most flexible.

- The puck should be a few feet away from your body and about two or three inches behind your front foot.

- Bring your stick back at least to the height of your waist. Some prefer to hold the stick almost vertical.

- Keeping your eye on the puck, bring the stick down so that it hits the ice approximately one inch (2.5 cm) behind the puck. Follow through and aim your stick blade where you want the puck to go.

- Start out slow and focus on contact. Then add speed and power as your accuracy improves.

Weber exerts tremendous pressure on his stick as he blasts his slap shot.

Weber is known as a great defenseman. But he contributes more than his share of offense. Weber has had multiple 20-goal seasons and was fourth in points for the Predators in 2015–16. Much of his scoring is due to his powerful slap shot.

At the 2015 NHL All-Star Skills Competition, Weber won the hardest-shot contest. His slap shot traveled 108.5 miles per hour (175 km/h). Weber's shot has left holes in boards and torn through nets. Players who try to block his shot end up paying the price in bruises or broken bones.

BOBBY HULL

Bobby Hull of the Chicago Blackhawks was called "The Golden Jet." With his blond hair and 30-mile-per-hour (48-km/h) skating speed, he was a golden blur on the ice. Hull's slap shot was just as hard to see. It was once clocked at 118 miles per hour (190 km/h). Hull played in an era when many goalies didn't wear masks. His slap shot likely helped change the minds of many of them. Hull scored his 51st goal of the 1965–66 season with his slap shot. He was the first player in NHL history to score more than 50 goals in a season.

Weber shows off his form in the hardest-shot contest at the NHL All-Star Skills Competition.

Weber stands 6 feet 4 inches (193 cm) and weighs
235 pounds (107 kg), so his size helps provide some of the
power behind his slap shot. But he credits practice and
technique for making his shot effective.

On his slap shot, Weber brings the stick back so it's
almost straight up in the air. While his upper body is
strong, he remains flexible in his
hips. That flexibility helps him
transfer his weight through the
shot and get incredible power on
it. Weber keeps his eye on the puck
until just before contact. Then he focuses on the target,
allowing him to pick out where he wants to hit it.

Nashville traded Weber to the Montreal Canadiens on June 29, 2016.

DRILL DOWN!

This drill works on slap-shot accuracy.

1. Find a block of wood that's roughly 12 inches (30 cm) on each side.

2. Place the block at a comfortable shooting distance.

3. Take slap shots at the block, trying to hit it and hit it with power.

4. See how far and straight you can drive the block with the puck.

PLAY DEFENSE LIKE

DREW DOUGHTY

As a defenseman for the Los Angeles Kings, Drew Doughty isn't afraid of going into the corners. He works hard to win the puck back for his team. And he's got the offensive skills to kick-start the Kings the other way. Doughty makes a perfect outlet pass to a teammate. Then he follows the play. He waits for a pass. Then he wrists it into the corner of the net. Doughty plays defense, but his offense can turn the game around in an instant.

Doughty grew up in London, Ontario, Canada, playing hockey and soccer. He played goalie in soccer and was able to look over the entire field and see plays develop. That helped him later as a hockey defenseman. Doughty became a star in junior

Doughty won Olympic gold medals with Team Canada in Vancouver in 2010 and Sochi, Russia, in 2014.

Defenseman Drew Doughty is an important part of the Los Angeles Kings' offense.

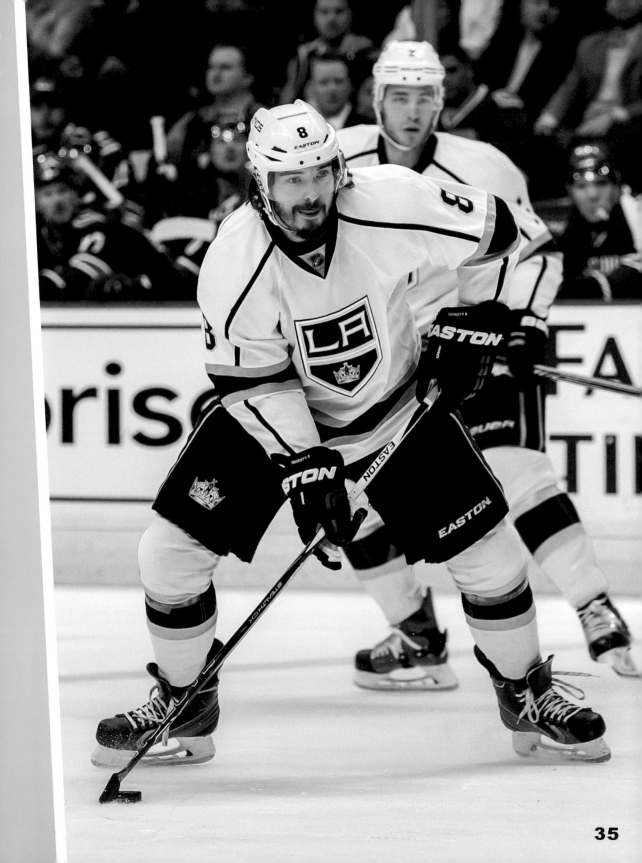

hockey. He was considered the top defenseman in the 2008 NHL Draft. The Kings chose him second overall.

Doughty was a key part of the Kings' first two Stanley Cup champions. He sees a lot of ice time. He plays on the power play, and he kills penalties. Doughty's ability to study the play helps him to be in the right place at the

PLAY DEFENSE LIKE DREW DOUGHTY

- Keep your feet moving. Forwards will skate circles around you if you are flat-footed and stationary.

- Play between the faceoff dots. That will push attackers to the outside and keep you between the puck and the net.

- Keep your stick on the ice when defending the puck carrier. You could deflect an attempted shot or pass, or you could knock the puck away. Remember, "stick on stick, body on body."

- Remember to communicate. Let your defensive partner know what's heading his way. Keep the goalie informed on puck location. Tell your forwards which players to pick up when the opponent attacks. And be loud!

Doughty holds the Norris Trophy in 2016 after he won it for the first time.

right time. He plays with confidence. He doesn't rush and make bad decisions.

If Doughty does make a mistake, he can quickly catch up and try to fix it. Early in his career in a game against the Detroit Red Wings, he carried the puck up the ice during a power play. He lost the puck at the Red Wings blue line, giving Detroit's Pavel Datsyuk a shorthanded chance going the other way. But Doughty chased him down and kept Datsyuk from shooting.

Doughty led all NHL defensemen in goals and assists in the 2012 Stanley Cup Playoffs.

NICKLAS LIDSTRÖM

Teammates called Nicklas Lidström "Mr. Perfect." He just seemed to do everything well. The Detroit Red Wings defenseman shut down opponents. But Lidström also could score, he didn't take many penalties, and he rarely missed games. He was a gifted skater and student of the game. Lidström seemed to know where the puck was going before it was passed. He played with the Red Wings from 1991 to 2012. He was selected for 11 All-Star games and won seven Norris Trophies as the NHL's best defenseman.

DRILL DOWN!

This drill helps you work on the transition from forward to backward skating.

1. Set up two cones a few feet apart at the top of a faceoff circle.

2. Start at one of the cones and skate backward to the bottom of the circle. Then switch to forward skating back to the top.

3. Go around the cone, and skate backward to the bottom of the circle the way you came.

4. Switch to forward skating back to the top of the circle, go around that cone, and repeat.

STICKHANDLE LIKE

PATRICK KANE

When Patrick Kane carries the puck into the offensive zone, defenders are on alert. With his stickhandling ability, there's no telling what he'll do next. Just when it looks as if he's going to shoot, he stops, slides the puck to his right, and goes around a defender. Kane spins around another opponent, keeping the puck glued to his stick. Then it's just him and the goalie. He picks out the top corner, waits for the goalie to commit, and fires. There's a reason they call Kane "Showtime."

Kane won the Stanley Cup for the Blackhawks in 2010 with his overtime goal in Game 6.

Growing up in Buffalo, New York, Kane was rarely without a hockey stick. What he used for a puck varied. Wherever he went, he practiced his stickhandling.

Patrick Kane keeps his eyes on the puck as he stickhandles through traffic.

Kane even practiced in the hallways of hotels when traveling for tournaments. He played all the time, sometimes hundreds of games per season. His work ethic and love for the game paid off. The Chicago Blackhawks made him the first pick of the 2007 NHL draft. Kane won his third Stanley Cup in Chicago in 2015, and he was the MVP of the playoffs in 2013.

STICKHANDLE LIKE PATRICK KANE

- Focus on controlling the puck, not just moving it from side to side. Use the space in front of and behind you to keep the puck away from your opponent.

- Keep your body hand (the one holding the end of the stick) in front of you, not off to the side. That will give you more lateral range of motion.

- Use your head and shoulders to deke and get past defenders.

- As you gain confidence, try more advanced moves such as the toe drag or spin move.

- Place your body between your opponent and the puck to protect it as you get closer to the net.

Kane uses his reach to keep the puck away from a defender.

At 5-foot-11 (180 cm) and 180 pounds (82 kg), Kane is smaller than most NHL defensemen. But his opponents can't hit him if they can't catch him. Kane is fast and can change direction quickly. But those

Kane led the NHL in points for the first time in 2016.

skating skills would be nothing without his stickhandling. Kane rarely loses the puck, despite all his movement. Defensemen have to respect his speed. That gives him space either to make a move or pass to a teammate.

Kane has what NHL scouts call "soft hands." When the puck is on his stick, he can keep it there. That lets him use his speed without worrying about losing the puck.

PAVEL BURE

Pavel Bure was a star in the Soviet Union before coming to the NHL. At the age of 19, he scored 35 goals in 44 games with his team in Moscow. When scouts went to see him play, they couldn't believe his amazing stickhandling and speed. Bure earned the nickname "The Russian Rocket." His career was cut short due to injury, but he still scored 437 goals in just 702 career NHL games.

DRILL DOWN!

This USA Hockey drill is great for improving stickhandling.

1. Take three objects (cones, gloves, or any similar-sized object) and put them in a triangle.

2. The point of the triangle should be four feet in front of you, with the two base points two feet to either side of you.

3. Move the puck around each cone without moving your feet. When that becomes easy, do it while skating.

4. Remember to keep your knees bent for better control. Always wear your hockey gloves when practicing stickhandling.

GLOSSARY

ASSIST

A pass or shot that sets up a teammate to score a goal.

BLADE

The part of the stick that handles the puck.

BLUE LINE

The line on the ice that establishes the offensive or defensive zone.

BREAKAWAY

A one-on-one opportunity for a skater against a goalie.

CREASE

The area in front of a goal—generally painted blue—where the goalie plays.

DRAFT

A system that allows teams to acquire new players coming into a league.

ONE-TIMER

When a player gets a pass and shoots the puck without it stopping.

OUTLET PASS

A pass made from the defensive zone to a teammate who is breaking into the neutral zone, often leading to a breakaway.

POWER PLAY

When a team plays with an extra attacker because of an opponent's penalty.

SHORTHANDED

When a team is missing a player due to penalty.

STRIDE

The motion of a player's legs while skating.

FOR MORE INFORMATION

BOOKS

Labrecque, Ellen. *The Science of a Slap Shot*. Ann Arbor, MI: Cherry Lake Publishing, 2016.

Nagelhout, Ryan. *The Science of Hockey*. New York: PowerKids Press, 2016.

Stuckey, Rachel. *Up Your Game On and Off the Ice*. New York: Crabtree Publishing Company, 2015.

WEBSITES

To learn more about hockey, visit **booklinks.abdopublishing.com**. These links are routinely monitored and updated to provide the most current information available.

PLACE TO VISIT

Hockey Hall of Fame
30 Yonge Street
Toronto, ON M5E 1X8, Canada
+1 (416) 360-7735
www.hhof.com
This hall of fame celebrates the history of hockey and its greatest players and contributors through memorabilia and other interactive exhibits. Among the highlights of the museum is the opportunity to view the original Stanley Cup trophy.

INDEX

Bishop, Ben, 12, 15–16
Bure, Pavel, 44

Crosby, Sidney, 18, 21–22,
    24–25

Datsyuk, Pavel, 38
Doughty, Drew, 34, 37–38

Hull, Bobby, 30

Kane, Patrick, 40, 43–44

Lemieux, Mario, 6
Lidström, Nicklas, 38

Orr, Bobby, 22
Ovechkin, Alex, 6, 9–10

Roy, Patrick, 16

Sakic, Joe, 10

Weber, Shea, 26, 29–30, 32

ABOUT THE AUTHOR

Todd Kortemeier studied journalism and English at the
University of Minnesota and has authored dozens of books for
young people, primarily on sports topics. He lives in
Minneapolis, Minnesota, with his wife.